The
Red Hat Society.
Night Before Christmas

The
Red Hat Society
Night Before Christmas

Illustrated by Sue Ellen Cooper,
Exalted Queen Mother
Story by Connie Goss Japsen

Gibbs Smith, Publisher

TO ENRICH AND INSPIRE HUMANKIND

Salt Lake City | *Charleston* | *Santa Fe* | *Santa Barbara*

First Edition
11 10 09 08 07   5 4 3 2 1

Published by
Gibbs Smith, Publisher
PO Box 667
Layton, Utah 84041

Orders: 1-800-835-4993
www.gibbs-smith.com

Designed by Black Eye Design, Inc.
Printed and bound in China

Library of Congress Cataloging-in-Publication Data

Japsen, Connie Goss.
The Red Hat Society night before Christmas / Connie Goss
Japsen ;
illustrations by Sue Ellen Cooper.—1st ed.
p. cm.
ISBN-13: 978-1-4236-0263-7
ISBN-10: 1-4236-0263-3
1. Santa Claus—Poetry. 2. Christmas—Poetry. 3. Red Hat
Society—Poetry. I. Cooper, Sue Ellen. II. Title.

PS3610.A66R43 2007
811'.6—dc22
                          2007009147

This book is dedicated to each and every
member of the Red Hat Society who has
answered the call to come out and play.

'Twas the day before Christmas; all through Santa's house
Not a creature was stirring, not even his spouse.
The toys were all finished and packed in his sleigh;
The reindeer were chewing their last lunch of hay
To ready themselves to deliver that night
All the gifts that were wished for, to children's delight.

Santa's workshop was silent; the elves were on break.

They'd worked hard all year for the good children's sake.

The old gent himself was curled up for a snooze,

So he'd be at his best for his "heavenly cruise"

Among all the stars in the bright Milky Way,

For the annual Christmas Eve visit he'd pay.

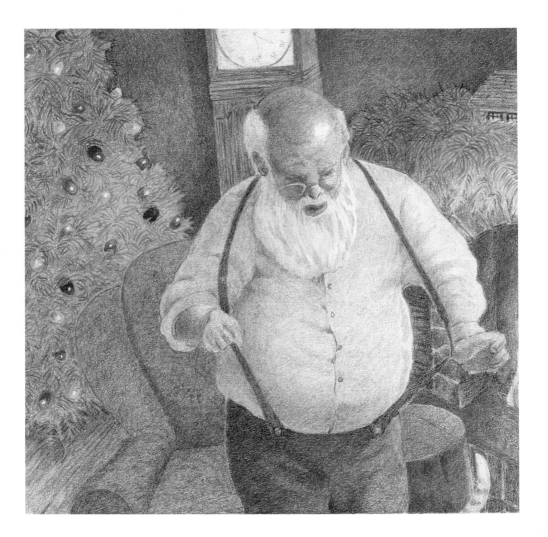

His dream ended abruptly; he woke with a jerk!

And exclaimed, "Oh my goodness! I must get to work!

I have to get ready; now, where is my cap?

I'm sure it was here when I lay down to nap."

He checked his suspenders, looked under his beard,

And wondered how his favorite cap disappeared!

He thought to himself, "Has my memory gone blurry?

If no toys are delivered, the children will worry!"

He'd ask Mrs. Santa. He called out her name.

Perhaps she'd not heard, because no answer came.

"I'll look in the closet—I'm sure Mrs. C

Would know where my cap is; she looks out for me."

All cleaned and pressed neatly, his **red** Christmas suits

Hung ready to wear, near his **shiny black boots.**

Mrs. Claus loved and cared for him so tenderly,

Surely she'd know where his red cap would be!

He peered high and low, even under the bed.

All he got for his search was a **bump** on his head!

But time was a-wasting—he called on his elves,

Who frantically searched all the cupboards and shelves.

They found cookies and candies and **goodies galore**

That the Missus had made—**but no cap was in store.**

DECEMBE
3
Donner 4
to vet
3:00
5
Bazaar 10
11
12
Yoga
class
17
18
19
Red Hat 24
Brunch
11:30
25
26
31

They started to fret; how they wished she were home!

And then an **idea** lit up old Santa's dome.

He looked at her **calendar**—he'd just had a hunch—

And on it she'd written "The Red Hatters' Brunch."

More rapid than eagles he dialed her cell phone;

Sure enough, Missus answered, "I'm on my way home.

I can't wait to tell you, but you have to see

What I wore for my hat at the Red Hatters' Tea!"

And in just a few minutes she came on her sled;

Santa's mouth dropped his pipe when he looked at her head!

For there was his cap looking strangely more jolly,

Sporting feathers of purple and red, and some holly.

"So that's where my cap went. I had such a tizzy!

I'm glad that you're home, but we have to get busy."

Mrs. Santa explained, "There's no need for alarm;

I went on a whim, and I meant you no harm.

For you were asleep and in such peaceful bliss

I'd no heart to wake you, so I blew you a kiss.

I borrowed your cap, but I added my touch.

All the girls at the tea liked my hat very much!"

Then Santa, relieved, said, "It's time that I go.

Help me change back the cap to the look people know.

I can't go without—risk a case of the sniffles;

The kids are awaiting their dolls, drums, and whistles."

So she pulled at the trim as she tried to unglue it;

With no luck, she cried, "There's no time to undo it!

"Can't you wear it as is? It looks really quite chic!

And I like how the feathers just brush past your cheek!

So what if you've now got a fancier bonnet!

It's what's in your cap and not what's upon it.

As your wife, I'm so proud; you do good things that matter;

And I think you might be the original Red Hatter!"

So Santa gave in, said, "I'll go with the flow—

But I'd better not see anybody I know."

The reindeer just stared at the cap all askew

Then they got into harness; they had work to do!

Santa winked and he shifted his new cap upright

As he sprang to his sleigh and then drove out of sight.

Mrs. Claus watched him **fly** through the cold North Pole weather

And saw the wind blow from his cap a red feather.

She watched as it **floated** and drifted away

To the far distant lands where the little kids play.

So, be on the lookout; you just never know—

You may find a **red feather** out there in the snow.

Mrs. Claus watched him **fly** through the cold North Pole weather

And saw the wind blow from his cap a red feather.

She watched as it **floated** and drifted away

To the far distant lands where the little kids play.

So, be on the lookout; you just never know—

You may find a **red feather** out there in the snow.